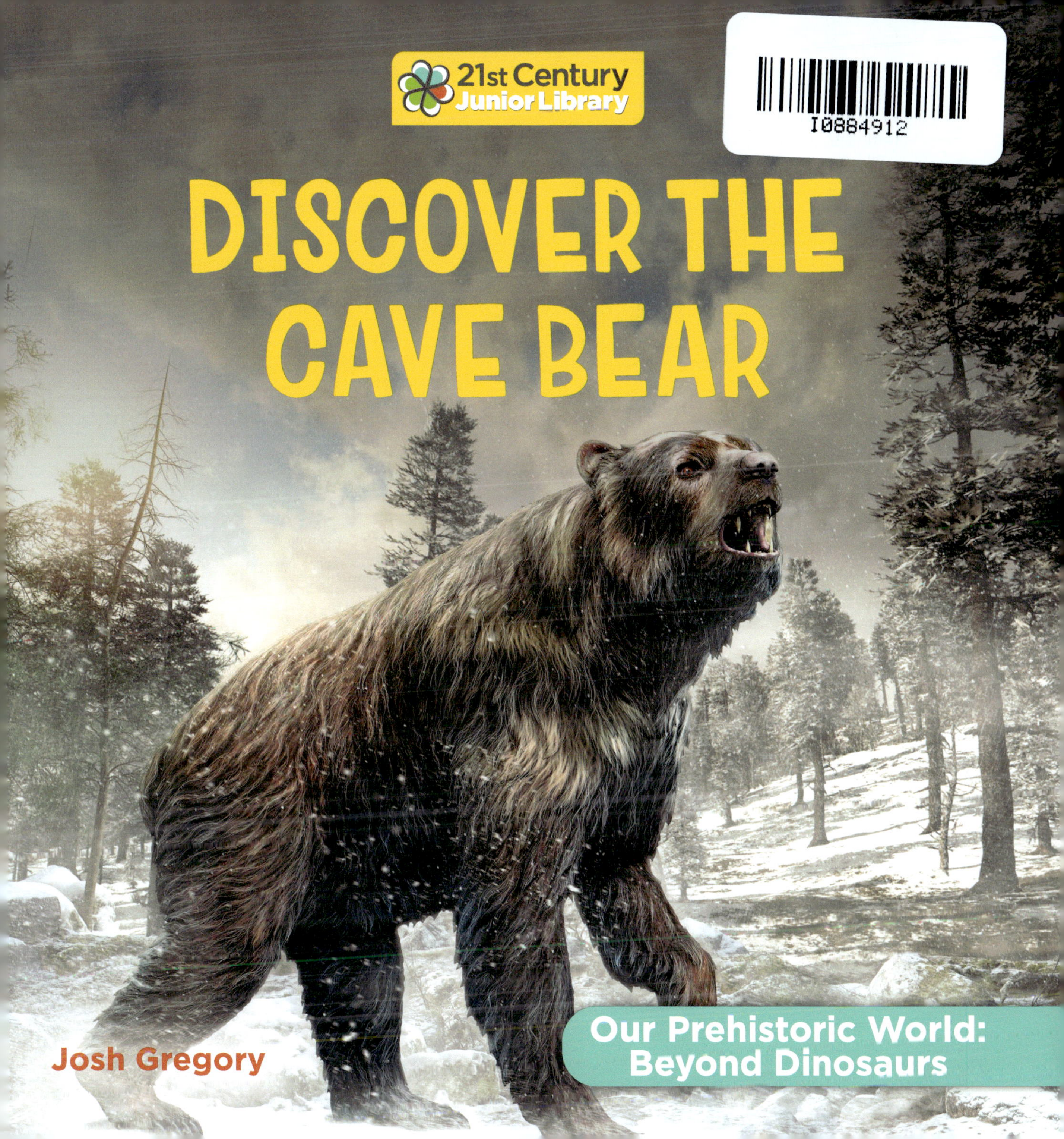

21st Century Junior Library

DISCOVER THE CAVE BEAR

Josh Gregory

Our Prehistoric World: Beyond Dinosaurs

Published in the United States of America by:

Cherry Lake Press
2395 South Huron Parkway, Suite 200, Ann Arbor, Michigan 48104
www.cherrylakepress.com

Reading Adviser: Beth Walker Gambro, MS, Ed., Reading Consultant, Yorkville, IL

Photo and Illustration Credits: © Warpaint/Shutterstock, cover, title page; Charles R. Knight, Public domain, via Wikimedia Commons, 5; © MLouisphotography/Alamy, 6; Fondo Antiguo de la Biblioteca de la Universidad de Sevilla from Sevilla, España via Wikimedia Commons, 7; © uchytel/Prehistoric Fauna Studio, 8–9; © Elvin Hamzayev/iStock.com, 10–11; © Danny Ye/Shutterstock, 12; © BlackFarm/Shutterstock, 13; © Defyclassic/Dreamstime.com, 14; James St. John via Wikimedia Commons, 16–17; Internet Archive Book Images, No restrictions, via Wikimedia Commons, 18–19; © Horia Bogdan/Shutterstock, 20

Cherry Lake Press is an imprint of Cherry Lake Publishing Group.

Library of Congress Cataloging-in-Publication Data has been filed and is available at catalog.loc.gov.

Cherry Lake Press would like to acknowledge the work of the Partnership for 21st Century Learning, a Network of Battelle for Kids. Please visit Battelle for Kids online for more information.

Printed in the United States of America

Cherry Lake Press

CONTENTS

WHAT WAS A CAVE BEAR?

You can find bears almost anywhere you go. Polar bears dash across Arctic ice. Pandas roam the mountains of China. Huge brown bears stalk the forests of North America and Europe. Bears have lived on Earth for more than 30 million years. And long ago, there were types of bears that no longer exist today.

Cave bears likely lived in groups, especially during **hibernation**.

One of the most famous prehistoric bears was the cave bear. This huge animal lived throughout much of what is now Europe. It was closely related to today's brown bears and polar bears. It probably went **extinct** about 24,000 years ago.

Climate change is likely what killed off cave bears. The plants they ate stopped growing where they lived.

Think!

What other kinds of animals have gone extinct? What do you know about them?

Cave bears got their name because they spent a lot of time in caves. The caves gave them shelter in cold, snowy weather. The bears lived during the Ice Age. During that time, sheets of ice covered big parts of Earth. The weather was often very cold.

Create!

Imagine you're running a winter hibernation spot for cave bears. Create a brochure for the caves you have available. Include the benefits of cave life and the food available in the area for the bears before they snuggle in for winter.

WHAT DID A CAVE BEAR LOOK LIKE?

Cave bears were huge. But they weren't any bigger than the large bear **species** that live today. Smaller cave bears weighed around 880 pounds (400 kilograms). Bigger ones reached up to 2,200 pounds (1,000 kg). That's about the size of a large polar bear or brown bear. Those are the largest bear species alive today.

Cave bears had steep, domed foreheads. This was to make room for large sinuses that helped them hibernate longer.

Cave bears also looked a lot like bears that live today. They had heavy, furry bodies. They mostly walked on four legs. They could probably stand up on their back legs if needed. Their heads were especially big. This meant there was room in their jaws for very big teeth. These were good for chewing tough plants.

The sharp front teeth on cave bears likely helped them tear leaves and branches off of plants.

Look!

With an adult, find videos of bears online or visit some at a zoo. Observe them. What do you notice about them?

Cave bears likely woke up from hibernation after the last of the harsh winter weather was gone.

HOW DID A CAVE BEAR LIVE?

Cave bears might have lived together in family groups. They shared caves when it was time to hibernate. This is when they settled down to sleep through the winter. They ate a lot of food to fatten up before hibernating. Then they stayed in their caves for months. Experts think cave bears hibernated for a longer time than today's bears do.

Modern bears eat to gain up to hundreds of pounds in the months before hibernation. Cave bears likely did the same.

Cave bears were **omnivores**. Their diet was mostly plants. They probably ate a lot of fruit, nuts, and leaves. But they could also hunt small animals. These big bears probably ate bugs and fish. They might have also eaten small **mammals**. But they didn't try to take down larger **prey**.

Make a Guess!

What else do you think a cave bear ate? Think about the foods today's bears eat.

Some cave bear fossil remains have shown slice marks and cracked bones. This may be proof that humans hunted the bears.

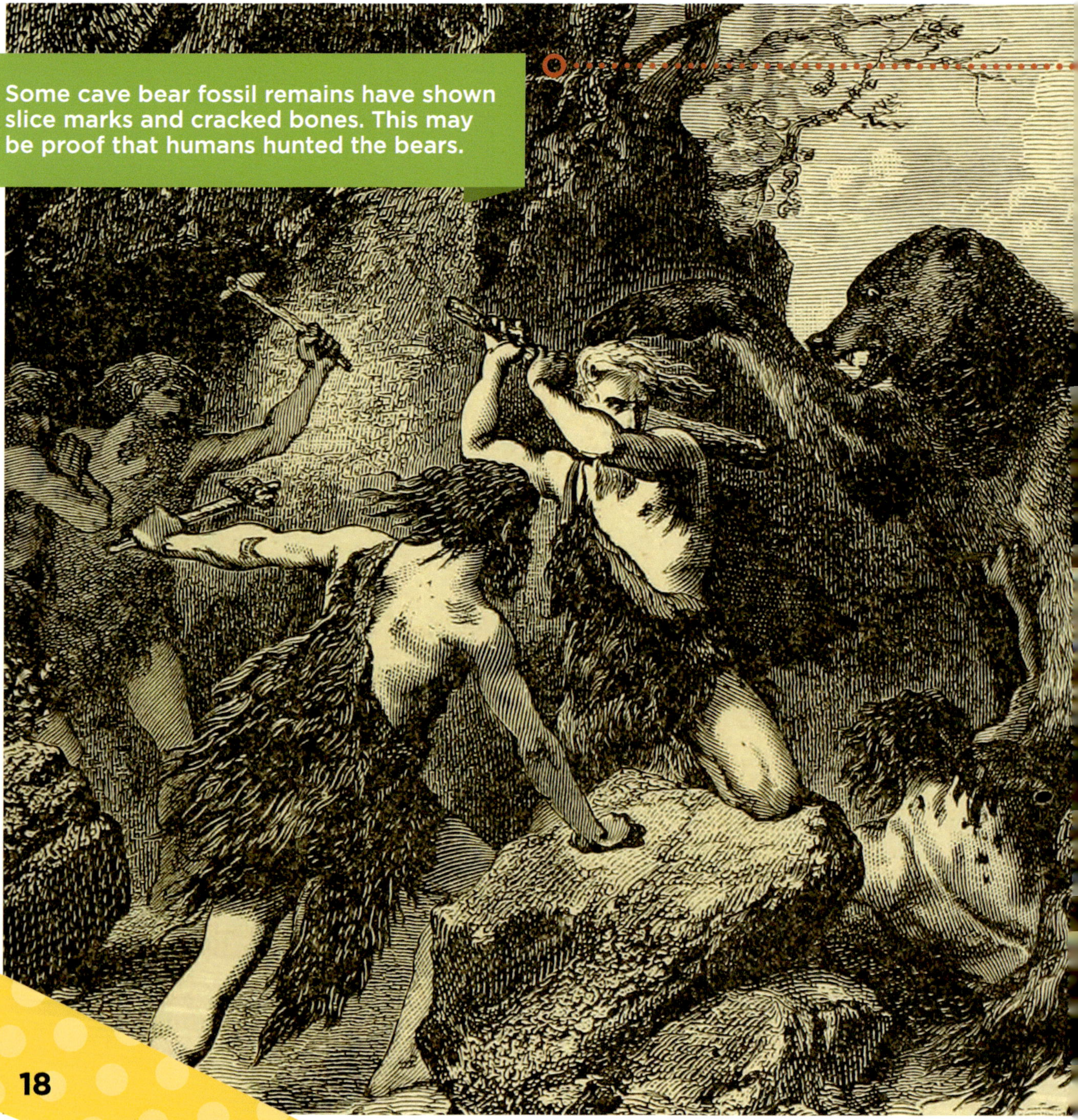

Adult cave bears probably didn't have many **predators**. They were too big and powerful. Other animals would have had a hard time hunting them. Sometimes a pack of wolves might have hunted a sick or old bear. Prehistoric humans sometimes hunted the bears, too. Scientists have found tools made from cave bear bones. They have also found paintings of cave bears.

Over 30,000 cave bears have been found in Drachenhöhle cave in Austria.

Scientists have uncovered **fossils** of more than 100,000 cave bears. These fossils have helped them learn about cave bears. Fossilized teeth help scientists learn what foods the bears ate. Fossilized bones tell them the bears' size. You can see these fossils at many museums around the world. It's the closest you'll come to meeting a real cave bear!

Ask Questions!

Is there something you want to know about cave bears? Try asking the experts at a museum. They will tell you what scientists know and don't know about cave bears.

GLOSSARY

extinct **(ik-STINKT)** no longer found living anywhere on Earth

fossils **(FAH-suhlz)** remains or traces of plants, animals, and other living things that have been preserved as rocks

hibernation **(hie-buhr-NAY-shuhn)** a period of long-term sleep during the winter

mammals **(MAA-muhlz)** warm-blooded animals that have hair and give birth to live young

omnivores **(AHM-nuh-vorz)** animals that eat both meat and plants

predators **(PREH-duh-terz)** animals that hunt other animals for food

prey **(PRAY)** animals that are hunted by other animals for food

species **(SPEE-sheez)** group of living things that share many characteristics and can mate and produce offspring

FIND OUT MORE

Books

Neuenfeldt, Elizabeth. *Cave Bears.* Minneapolis, MN: Bellwether Media, 2025.

Tite, Jack. *Mega Meltdown: The Weird and Wonderful Animals of the Ice Age.* New York, NY: Blueprint Editions, 2018.

Websites

With an adult, learn more online with these suggested searches.

Encyclopedia Britannica Kids: Cave Bear
Learn more about the cave bear and find out why some experts think they went extinct.

Atlas Obscura: Why Europe's Cave Bears Were—and Weren't—Made for Hunkering Down
Find out how scientists learned about the cave bear's hibernation habits.

INDEX

ABOUT THE AUTHOR

Josh Gregory is the author of more than 250 books for young readers, covering everything from video games and technology to dinosaurs and U.S. history. He lives in Chicago, Illinois.

About Paleoartists

Paleoartists bring the prehistoric world to life! They work with scientists, paleontologists, museums, and their own research to recreate living things from long, long ago. **Mark Witton** is one paleoartist featured in this series. He has been studying prehistoric creatures for over 20 years! **Brian Engh** is another. He builds sculptures, too. He designs and builds whole exhibits. He started Living Relic Productions.